BUSY LITTLE
GARDENER

HELEN BARDEN

ILLUSTRATED BY

PENNY DANN

JellyBean Press
New York

This book belongs to

Design: Alison Fenton
Design assistants: Karen Fenton
and Caroline Johnson
Editor: Sue Hook
Photography: Mike Galletly
Photograph (page 11): Annet Held

First published in 1990 by
Conran Octopus Limited
37 Shelton Street, London WC2H 9HN

© text 1990 Conran Octopus Limited
© illustration 1990 Penny Dann

This 1990 edition published by
JellyBean Press,
distributed by Outlet Book Company, Inc.,
a Random House Company,
225 Park Avenue South, New York, New York 10003

Printed and bound in Great Britain

ISBN 0-517-036037

87654321

Contents

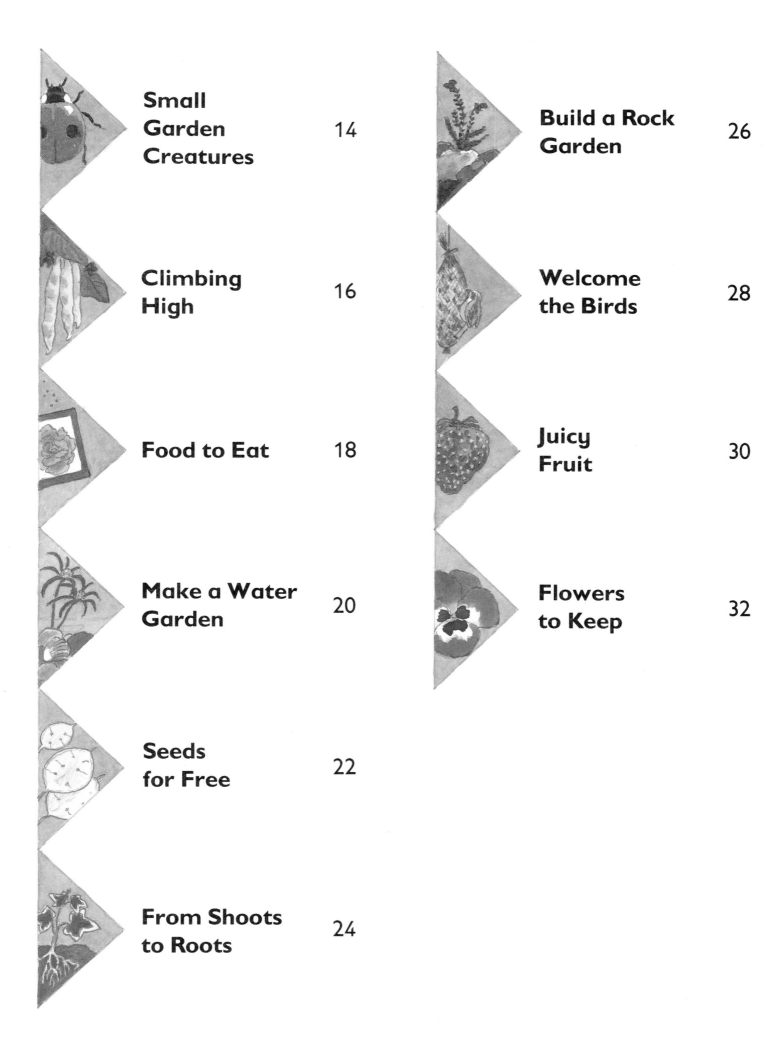

How to be a Gardener

The garden is a very exciting place. Lots of new and wonderful things happen in it all through the year. Gardeners think about plants they can grow and the creatures that share the garden. Ask an adult to help you whenever you see this sign ★.

▶ **Find out how you can be a gardener**

Look at the many kinds of plants that will grow in a garden. Like us, all plants need food, water, light and lots of love.

A good gardener is a neat gardener. After working in the garden put all your tools away and always remember to wash your hands.

Plants need our help. We have to take care of them and learn how to watch and wait while they grow. Sometimes it takes a long time.

Are you ready to be a gardener?

Growing Beans

We are going to grow some beans.

You will need

string bean seeds

jar

pitcher of water

desk blotter paper

empty yogurt cup

1 Put a yogurt cup upside down in the jar. Roll the paper round like a tube and push it down into the jar round the yogurt cup. The cup will keep the paper in place.

2 Plant 3 or 4 beans between the paper and the wall of the jar. Don't let them fall to the bottom.

3 Pour in water to ¼ way up the jar. Place it somewhere warm and sunny.

4 Look at the beans every day and watch the roots and shoots grow.

A grow chart

Make a grow chart and tape it to the window near your growing beans. How many days was it before they began to grow? Which came first, shoots or roots?

5

Growing Seeds Indoors

Some seeds can be grown indoors. Try growing some alfalfa sprouts. They will grow very easily and very quickly.

You will need

alfalfa seeds   watering can

margarine tubs   cotton or potting soil

1 Put some cotton in the bottom of the margarine tub. Soak the cotton with water.

2 Shake some seeds on to the cotton. Spread them out.

3 ▶ Look at the seeds every day. Make sure the cotton stays wet. Your seeds need water to help them grow.

Try something different

You could grow some other seeds – mustard, flowers, bird seeds. Look at different seeds – apples, melons.

Try growing sprouts on paper towels instead of on cotton.

4 ▶ After about a week your sprouts will be ready to eat. They will have grown about 2 ins. Cut the sprouts off near the bottom of their stalks and add them to your sandwiches.

Green Hats

We don't always have to grow from seeds. Try growing from vegetables and watch how new shoots appear.

You will need

chopping board

blunt-tipped knife

container

carrot

pitcher of water

radish

parsnip

★ adult help

I'm going to grow the carrot and parsnip.

I shall grow the radish.

1 Choose some vegetables with green tops. Decide what you would like to grow.

2 ★ Ask for help to cut the vegetable tops off with the knife. Do this on the chopping board.

4 It won't be long till you see the vegetables sprouting green hats. How many days did each one take?

3 Arrange the vegetable tops on a saucer and pour some water around them.

More shoots

Other vegetables can grow shoots. Look at an old potato or onion that has been left for 2-3 weeks. How many shoots can you see? You could plant these in the garden. Maybe they will grow.

Watch the Wild Things Grow

As you watch your garden you will see flowers and plants growing that you did not plant. These are weeds, wild plants that may try to take over your garden. You must take out the ones shown in the pictures.

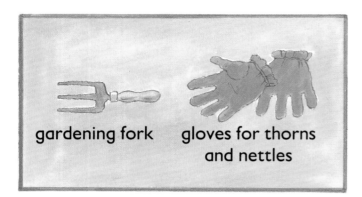

gardening fork

gloves for thorns and nettles

If we leave the roots the weeds will grow again.

I'm going to dig out all the roots.

2 Weeds grow very quickly. They have strong roots buried firmly in the soil. Weeding them out is very important but it's hard work!

Weeding is easier after a shower of rain.

My fork is helping me get the weeds out.

1 Try and pull out all the weeds from the soil before you sow. Weeds will steal the food, water and light that your plants need for growing.

I'm making a daisy chain.

Do you like butter?

3 Many weeds grow in the grass. Daisies, buttercups and dandelions are all weed flowers. They are wild flowers that like to spread across the grass.

Ground Elder

Ragwort

Coltsfoot

4 Look for vines and creepers. They will twist around and choke strong, healthy plants.

Make a wild garden. Leave a part of the soil bed empty for weeds to root themselves. Watch and see what will grow.

Did you know?..

Butterflies lay eggs on nettles.

You can make tea from dandelions.

Dock leaves can help ease a nettle sting.

What's the time dandelion clock?

One o'clock, two o'clock, three o'clock?

Dock Weed   Morning Glory   Wild Rose

A Giant Sunflower Race

Giant sunflowers grow very fast if you plant them in a sunny spot. In spring, have a race with a friend to see who can grow the tallest and biggest sunflower.

You will need

gardening fork   garden string

trowel   tape measure

sunflower seeds

garden stakes   watering can

1 Prepare a site near a fence or wall. Pull up any weeds and then dig and rake the soil with your fork.

3 Shoots will appear in about ten days if you water the seeds every day.

2 Push the seeds into the soil. Leave about 12 ins. between each one.

4 When the seedlings are about 2 ins. tall pull out the weak ones. Leave the strong ones to grow. Take any snails or slugs off the leaves.

5 Tie each sunflower to a garden stake to keep it from falling over. Measure your flower every day. It might grow 10-12 feet high.

Gardening tips

If you save some seeds you will be able to plant them next year.

Give some seeds to the birds in winter.

Small Garden Creatures

Lots of little creatures live in the garden. Some like to live in dark places, some like to be near the flowers and some bury themselves into the soil.

Many of these creatures are not friends of the gardener. Can you find any that help the gardener?

1 ▶ Have you seen the slugs nibbling through the leaves? They can kill many plants, so always pick them off the leaves when you see them. You could put them on the compost heap.

2 ▶ Ladybugs eat all the greenfly that will damage your roses. Good gardeners know the ladybug is a friend.

3 Caterpillars love eating lots of green vegetables. Make sure they don't eat yours.

4 Worms eat the soil and help make holes in the big lumps of soil. This makes digging easier for the gardener.

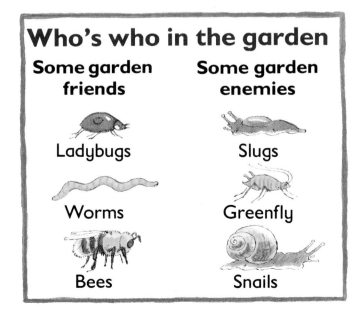

Who's who in the garden

Some garden friends	**Some garden enemies**
Ladybugs	Slugs
Worms	Greenfly
Bees	Snails

Let's have a snail race

Ready, set, go!
Which snail will get to the leaf first?

Climbing High

All plants grow upwards but many grow so high they need help to stand tall. These are climbing plants that like to grow up stakes, fences or trellis. Let's plant some string beans and watch them climb.

You will need

trellis or stakes

string bean seeds

trowel

garden twine

blunt-tipped scissors

★ adult help

1 First dig the stakes into the soil. Make 2 straight rows with your stakes. ★ Ask an adult to help as this is very difficult for little gardeners.

Climbing flowers

Other plants climb high too. Honeysuckle, clematis, sweet pea and climbing roses all look beautiful as they climb over a shed or fence in the garden. Try growing a climbing flower.

2 ★ Tie the stakes together at the top with your twine. Put a stake across the row of stakes and make very sure they are secure and strongly tied. The stakes must be very firm.

3 Dig a little hole with your trowel and sow 1 or 2 beans at the bottom of each stake.

4 String beans take a very long time to grow. All through the summer you can watch the plants grow round and curl up your stakes.

5 Little flowers appear on the plant and later these grow into string beans. When the beans look long enough to eat, pick them for your dinner.

Don't forget to keep watering the beans.

Food to Eat

Most of the food we eat is grown from seeds. Let's try to grow a salad using different vegetable seeds.

You will need

salad vegetable seeds

labels

pencil

marker sticks

string

gardening fork and trowel

watering can

wooden spoon

My fork is helping me crumble the soil.

Crumbly soil makes it easier for the seeds to grow.

1 Make sure the soil has no weeds or big stones in it. Dig the soil with the fork or trowel and break it into small lumps of earth.

I'll hold down the string this end with a marker.

I'll dig a line with the wooden spoon handle.

2 Use your string and marker sticks to mark a line ready for digging. With the wooden spoon handle dig a long trench about ¾ in. deep beside the string.

3 ▷ Gently shake your seeds into your trench. Space them out from each other. Sow lots of seeds because some might not grow. Have a different row for each vegetable.

4 ▷ Carefully water the seeds with your watering can. Cover the seeds with soil and firmly press it down with your feet. Water the row again.

5 ▷ It will take a long time until your vegetables are ready to eat. They will need lots of watering to help them grow. Keep going to look at them.

Make your own salad

Now you have grown some vegetables wash them well and make a salad. Don't forget to wash your hands first. You could add chopped apple and raisins or make a meal with a baked potato and grated cheese.

Make a Water Garden

Some plants like to grow in or very near to water. Ponds and lakes are home to many beautiful flowers and reeds. Make your own water garden like this.

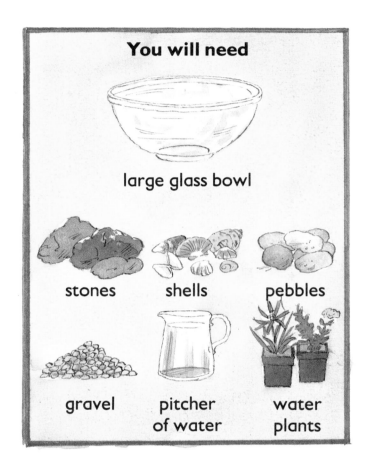

You will need

large glass bowl

stones   shells   pebbles

gravel   pitcher of water   water plants

1 Collect some beautiful stones, pebbles and shells of different shapes and sizes. Look for unusual colors and markings.

2 Arrange your collection in the bottom of the glass bowl.

3 Plant your water plants in small pots of soil. Put some gravel on top of the soil to keep it from washing away.

Reflections

Cover a jar lid with aluminium foil and put it at the bottom of your water garden. What can you see?

Hide the pot among the pebbles.

We can't forget to change the water each week.

Clean water helps the plants stay healthy.

4 Put your plants among the heavy stones. Make sure they are secure, so the plants do not tip over.

5 Slowly pour in the water from the pitcher to cover the pots and pebbles.

Change the water once a week. Use your pitcher to scoop out the old water so that you don't disturb your garden.

Seeds for Free

Many plants carry their seeds inside their fruit or flower. When the seeds are ready they burst out or are blown to new places and will grow again. The seed pods look dead and very dry. Can you find some free seeds?

You will need

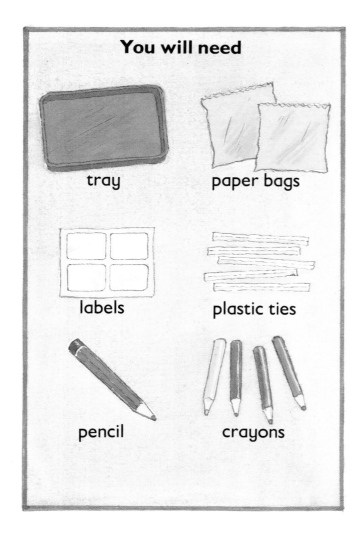

tray

paper bags

labels

plastic ties

pencil

crayons

1 Look for seed pods in the garden, or ask Mom or Dad to look with you in woods and fields. Collect as many as you can.

2 Carefully lay each seed pod on a tray. Try to name each one.

> I can hear the seeds falling into the bag.

> I'm going to open up this pod to see the seeds.

3 Put each seed pod into one of the paper bags and shake very gently. Do it slowly. Seed pods are very fragile.

> Next year we can plant these sweet peas again.

> Mommy can write the names on the bags.

4 Tie and label each bag ready to sow next year. Keep them somewhere cool and dry.

Falling seeds

Trees also make seeds for planting. In the fall hunt for acorns, chestnuts and sycamore wings. All of them are falling tree seeds. Play the sycamore wing game. Drop the wings from as high as you can and watch how long it takes for them to twirl to the ground.

With some of your seed pod collection you could make a decoration to last all winter.

From Shoots to Roots

In late spring and through summer you can grow new plants from healthy old ones. Take some cuttings from potted plants or outdoor shrubs. Take 3 or 4 cuttings from each plant.

You will need

safety scissors

root stimulator

bag of potting soil

flowerpots

watering can

pencil

labels

★ adult help

2 Choose strong young shoots, 2-4 ins. long. Count the places where the leaves join the stem. These are leaf joints. Your cuttings will need 2 leaf joints each.

3 ★ Take your cuttings. Cut as neatly as you can. Dip the end of each stem in root stimulator.

1 Fill the flowerpots with soil. Water them gently and make 3 or 4 little holes in the soil ready for your cuttings. Use the end of your pencil to make the holes.

Share your shoots

Your cuttings will grow roots in a few weeks if they are kept in a cool place and you water them regularly. Share them with your friends and visitors. Ask them to bring their plant cuttings to you and trade your collection.

4 ▶ Gently plant the stems of your cuttings into the soil. Keep the different types of plants separate. Make sure you have buried the stems well and made them secure. Label each pot.

Build a Rock Garden

There are plants that don't need much soil in which to grow. They can be grown in a rock garden, a garden made from rocks and stones where the plants and flowers grow over the rocks. Try making a little indoor rock garden.

1 Collect some large stones or rocks. Choose different sizes and shapes. Look for some moss and unusual pieces of wood to use, too.

2 Spread newspaper on the floor. Put some gravel in the bottom of your container. Now cover the gravel with soil. Make it as deep as your little finger.

You will need

old dishpan or container

bag of gravel

pieces of wood

bucket of soil

plants

rocks or stones

trowel

moss

newspaper

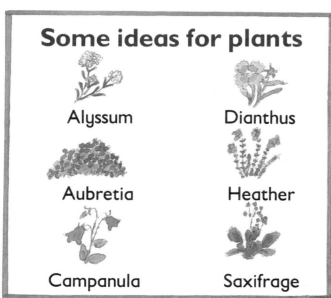

Some ideas for plants

Alyssum

Dianthus

Aubretia

Heather

Campanula

Saxifrage

3 Arrange the rocks and stones on the soil. Put the rocks close together leaving little spaces for your plants.

4 Plant your rock plants in the spaces. Push them down well to cover the roots with soil and make them secure.

5 Place your rock garden on a sunny windowsill. Make sure that your plants have enough water.

Welcome the Birds

The plants and flowers share the garden with other living things. Birds like to come and visit. Make a bird feeder for the birds in your garden.

You will need

bacon fat

nuts

mixing bowl

net fruit or vegetable bag

bread

lard

suet

blunt-tipped knife

string

rubber band or plastic tie

★ adult help

raisins

wooden spoon

Spot the birds

Which birds can you see today?

wren

pigeon

thrush

sparrow

blackbird

1　★ Cut up all the bacon and bread into small pieces. Ask for some help when using the knife.

2　Put the bacon and the bread into a bowl with the suet, raisins and nuts. Mix it all together.

3　Now add a tablespoon of lard and stir it in until the mixture sticks together in lumps.

4　Open the net bag and spoon the bird mixture into it until the bag is full. Tie the top with a rubber band or a plastic tie.

5　Tie some string to the bird feeder and hang it in the garden. Put it near a window so you can watch the visiting birds.

Look and learn

Which is the greediest bird?

Which bird comes with lots of friends?

Look for a bird that visits every day.

Have you made a bird friend?

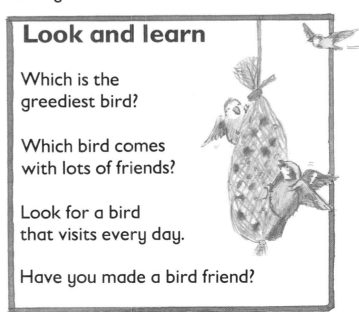

Juicy Fruit

Some of the fruit we like to eat can be grown in the garden. Fruits such as raspberries, blackberries and redcurrants can give lots of fruit in the summer. Let's grow some juicy red strawberries for a delicious summer snack.

You will need

strawberry seeds

watering can

seed trays

trowel

potting soil

pencil/labels

netting

1 In early spring sow your strawberry seeds in little seed trays. Fill the trays with soil and water it well.

3 Keep watching your seeds and water them when the soil starts to get dry. Wait to see the little shoots appear.

2 Shake a few seeds on to the soil in each tray and put the trays in a warm sunny place indoors. Write a label for each tray of seeds.

4 After about six weeks, when your little shoots look strong enough, gently dig them up. Plant each seedling in a sunny part of the garden, or in a pot or window box where you can watch them.

5 Your plants will flower and the flowers will turn into fruit. Birds like to eat strawberries so as the fruit starts to ripen protect the plants with netting.

6 When your strawberries are red and ripe gently pick them and wash them ready for eating.

Plant some pits

Pits from inside some fruit are seeds. Try planting apple or orange pits in little pots and see what happens. Could you try to grow an avocado pit too? It may sprout a shoot.

Flowers to Keep

You can have lots of fun collecting, drying and pressing flowers from your garden. Give a bunch of dried flowers to someone you love, or make pretty greetings cards with pictures made from flowers you have pressed.

▶ How to dry flowers

Pick the flowers on a dry, sunny day, when the petals are all open. Choose the best ones, with long stems.

★ Carefully cut off the leaves. Spread the flowers on paper towels on a tray. Don't let them touch each other.
★ Put them somewhere cool, dry and airy, away from sunlight. They will be ready to use in a few days.

Good flowers for drying

lavender   hydrangea   statice
and any pretty seed pods.

▶ How to press flowers

Put your flowers between 2 paper towels. Put 1 or 2 telephone books on top. Leave for about 4 weeks before removing the flowers.

Now make framed cards with paper stuck on to a larger sheet of cardboard. Glue a cut-out vase shape in place then add 2 or 3 pressed flowers. Write a greeting underneath with a colored pencil or felt-tip pen.

Good flowers for pressing

pansy   larkspur   daisy
and any pretty grasses and ferns.